"Please use coloured pencils instead of markers to colour in this book. Markers may bleed through the pages and ruin other designs. Thank you for helping to keep the book in good condition!"

This book

BELONGS TO

EMMA

EMMA

TABLE OF CONTENTS

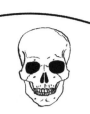

Anatomy for Kids

Introduction

Have you ever wondered how your body works and what interesting things are inside it?
What do your organs do?
Or where do babies come from?
Make the most of this book now that you have it. It will show you an easy way to learn through colouring. You will learn everything you need to know and even more!
Also, in the end, you can take a small test to see how much you've learned.

How to use this colouring book:
Match human organs with the names of human systems.
For example, lungs -> respiratory system.
Colour the organs and body parts that go with them on each page.
While colouring, say the names of the organs out loud.
Then, look at the pictures of the organs and try to picture where they are in your body, then try to locate them.

I. Human organs and their functions

Look at the diagram below to see where the organs are before you move on to learning about them.

Human Internal Organs

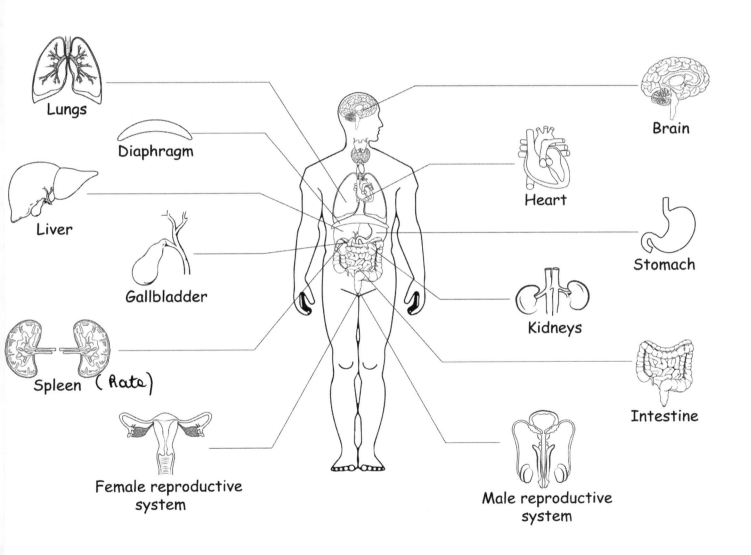

Lungs

Diaphragm

Liver

Gallbladder

Spleen (Rate)

Female reproductive system

Brain

Heart

Stomach

Kidneys

Intestine

Male reproductive system

Here we go ;)

Brain

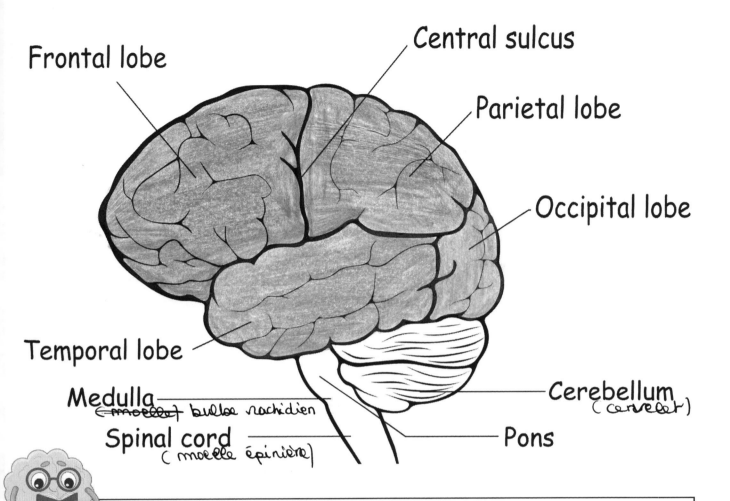

Frontal lobe

Central sulcus

Parietal lobe

Occipital lobe

Temporal lobe

Medulla <del>(moelle)</del> bulbe rachidien

Spinal cord (moelle épinière)

Cerebellum (cervelet)

Pons

The brain is in our heads and looks like a walnut. It is part of the nervous system. It controls everything you do, including what you think, say, hear, feel, move, and breathe. It also helps you remember things and decide what to do.
The cerebral hemispheres are the two parts of the brain that make up each half.
The right cerebral hemisphere makes us think about things like music and art. It also helps us show how we feel and recognise faces.
The left cerebral hemisphere helps us understand maths, speak, and think logically.

The external layer of the cerebral hemispheres is named the cerebral cortex.   ⟶ couche
It goes up and down in sharp waves and has furrows in it. The cortex is split into   ⟶ pointu   ⟶ sillon
lobes by deep grooves. The centres of the lobes do the following things: ⟶ profond   ⟶ rainure

- Frontal lobe - memory, thinking, movement, behaviour
- Parietal lobe - touch, language
- Temporal lobe -hearing, feelings, learning
- Occipital lobe - sight. (vue)

walnut = noyer (noix)

6

Heart

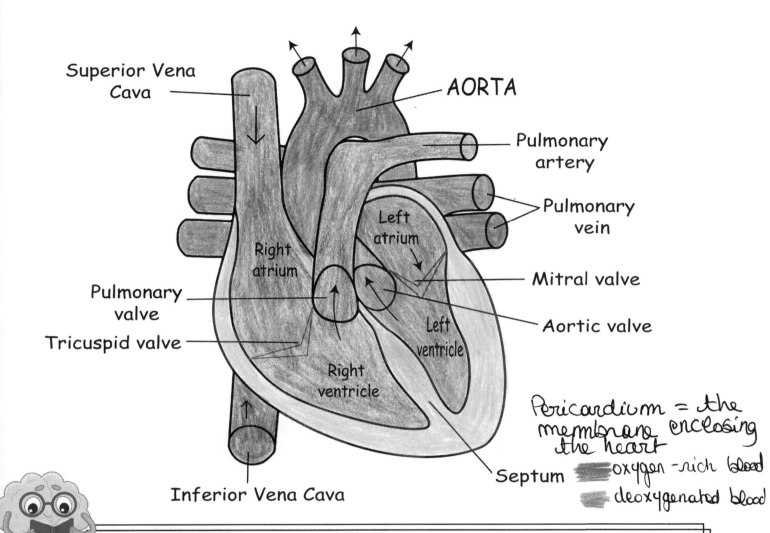

Superior Vena Cava

AORTA

Pulmonary artery

Pulmonary vein

Left atrium

Right atrium

Mitral valve

Pulmonary valve

Tricuspid valve

Aortic valve

Left ventricle

Right ventricle

Septum

Inferior Vena Cava

Pericardium = the membrane enclosing the heart

oxygen-rich blood

deoxygenated blood

The heart is the <u>muscle that pumps blood</u> to all parts of the body. Through <u>veins</u> and <u>arteries</u>, blood moves through our bodies and <u>brings oxygen</u> and <u>nutrients</u> to them. It is about as <u>big as a fist</u>. It is the most important part of the <u>circulatory system</u> and is found between the lungs in the chest.

There are two atriums and two ventricles in the heart. The muscle pumps blood from the <u>right atrium</u> into the <u>right ventricle</u>. The blood comes from the body through the right atrium. From there, the <u>blood</u> is pumped to the lungs, which take in oxygen and release carbon dioxide. The <u>oxygen-rich blood</u> then goes back to the heart through the left atrium, and the left ventricle pumps it into the body.

On each side of the heart, there are also <u>two valves</u>. Their job is <u>to stop the blood from going in the wrong direction</u>. A <u>septum</u> separates the <u>chambers of the</u> heart. It keeps oxygen and carbon dioxide from mixing in the blood, so the <u>tissues</u> get more oxygen from the blood. The <u>pericardium covers the heart</u>. This <u>keeps the muscle from contact with other organs and keeps the heart in the right place.</u>

release = libérer

Lungs

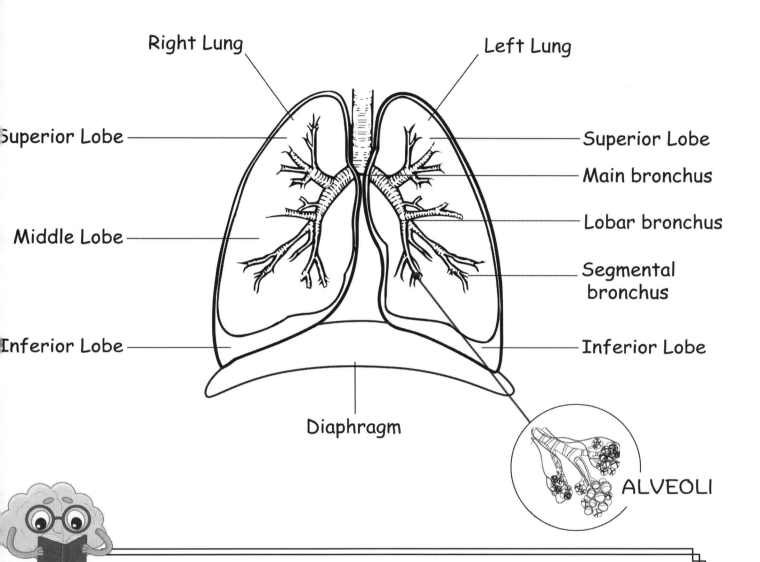

Right Lung

Left Lung

Superior Lobe

Superior Lobe

Main bronchus

Lobar bronchus

Middle Lobe

Segmental bronchus

Inferior Lobe

Inferior Lobe

Diaphragm

ALVEOLI

   Lungs are our body's organs responsible for breathing (part of the respiratory system). They are composed of the left lung (which has 2 lobes) and right lung (which has 3 lobes) and connect to the trachea and throat.

   The lungs consist of small air bubbles called **ALVEOLI**. When you breathe in through your nose or mouth, the air goes through your throat and trachea into your lungs. From there, it goes through your airways and into your alveoli.

   In the alveoli, gases from the air and the blood exchange places. Oxygen, which is necessary for life, gets into the blood, and carbon dioxide, a waste product of respiration, leaves the body.

Thyroid Gland

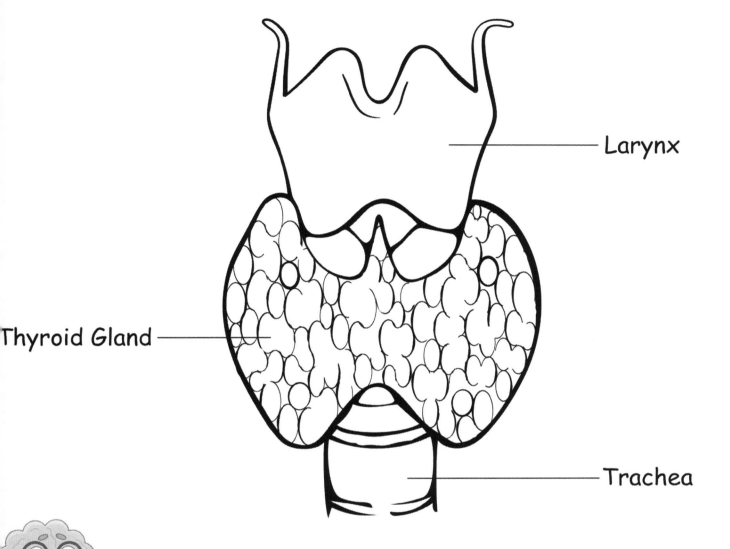

Larynx

Thyroid Gland

Trachea

The thyroid gland is the largest gland in the endocrine system. It looks like a butterfly. It is at the base of our neck, below our larynx. It has a very strong effect on our bodies, health, and even mood.

The thyroid gland makes hormones and sends them into the blood. These hormones control how our bodies work. These hormones are very important for digestion and metabolism, which is how our bodies turn food into energy. They also help control our body temperature. Depending on the weather, we feel hot or cold.

The gland also changes how we feel and how much we weigh. We feel good and have more energy when the thyroid is working well.

Liver

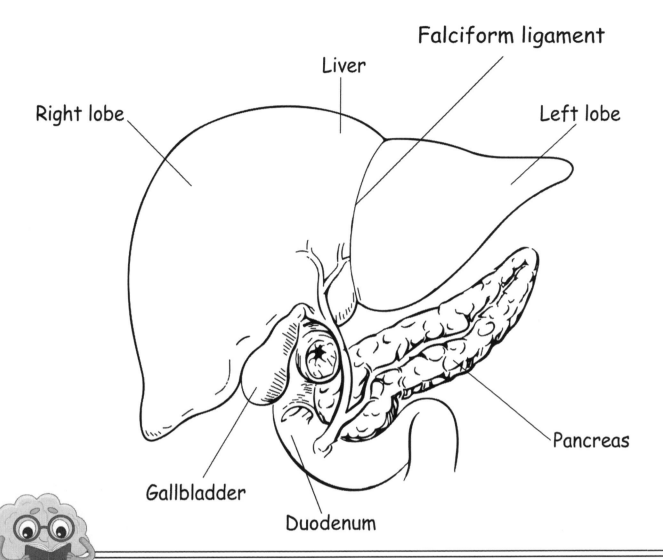

Liver

Falciform ligament

Right lobe

Left lobe

Pancreas

Gallbladder

Duodenum

The liver is part of the digestive system and one of the body's largest glands. It's located on the right side of the abdomen. The reddish-brown colour of the liver comes from how well the blood flows through it. It is a tough and strong organ that can even heal itself if it gets hurt.

The liver:

- Filters and cleans the blood to get rid of toxins and other harmful substances that can make us sick.
- It also makes bile, which helps us digest food by breaking down fat.
- Stores important vitamins and minerals.
- Controls blood sugar levels.
- And makes proteins that help blood clot when we cut ourselves.

Stomach

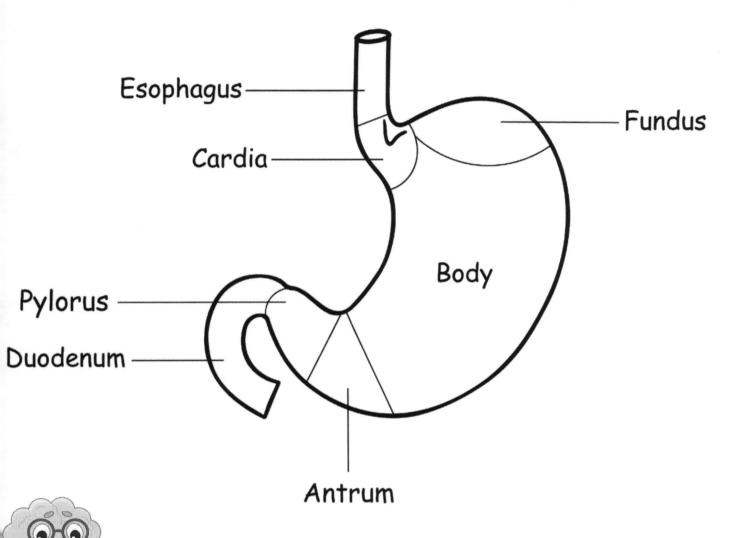

Esophagus

Fundus

Cardia

Body

Pylorus

Duodenum

Antrum

    The stomach lies on the left side of the upper abdomen under the diaphragm. It is shaped like a pouch and connects at the top to the esophagus and the bottom to the small intestine. It is a part of the digestive system that helps the body break down and absorb food.

    Food goes from the mouth to the stomach through the esophagus when we eat. In the stomach, it mixes with gastric juices, which help break down the food. The stomach's walls then tighten, which helps the food and gastric juices mix to make a thick liquid called food content. Food slowly moves from the stomach to the small intestine, where it is further broken down, and nutrients are absorbed into the body.

Kidneys

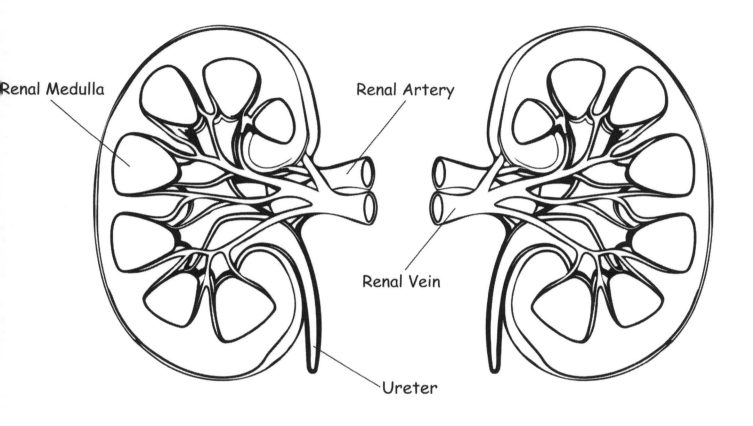

Renal Medulla

Renal Artery

Renal Vein

Ureter

The kidneys are two small organs shaped like beans. They are on either side of the spine in the lower back. They are part of the excretory system. The left kidney is higher than the right kidney.

The kidney's main job is removing waste and extra water from the blood. This waste and water are then passed out of the body through urine. The body's balance of fluids and electrolytes is also kept in check by these organs, which is important for our health.

Gallbladder

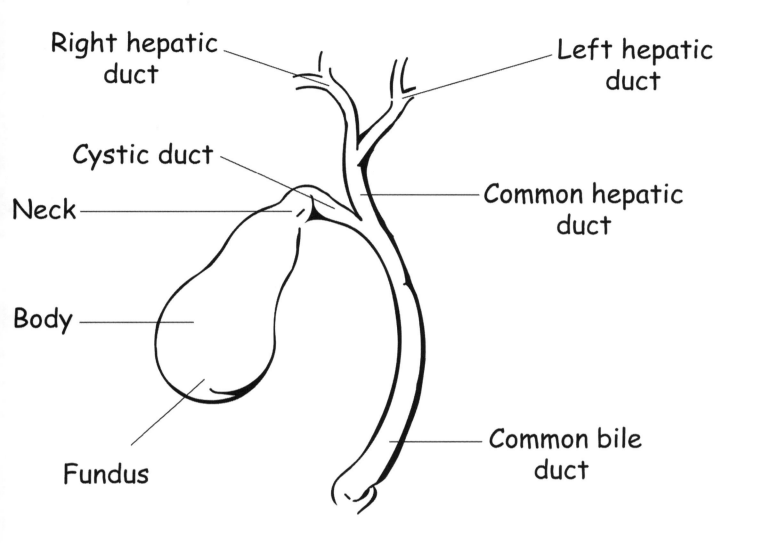

Right hepatic
duct

Left hepatic
duct

Cystic duct

Neck

Common hepatic
duct

Body

Common bile
duct

Fundus

The gallbladder is shaped like a pear and sits under the liver. The bile that our liver makes is stored in this organ. Bile helps our bodies break down fat and other foods. The gallbladder sends bile into the small intestine when we eat. This helps break down the food.

Along with bile, the body gets rid of cholesterol, drugs, toxins, bile acids, and other things that are bad for us.

Intestines

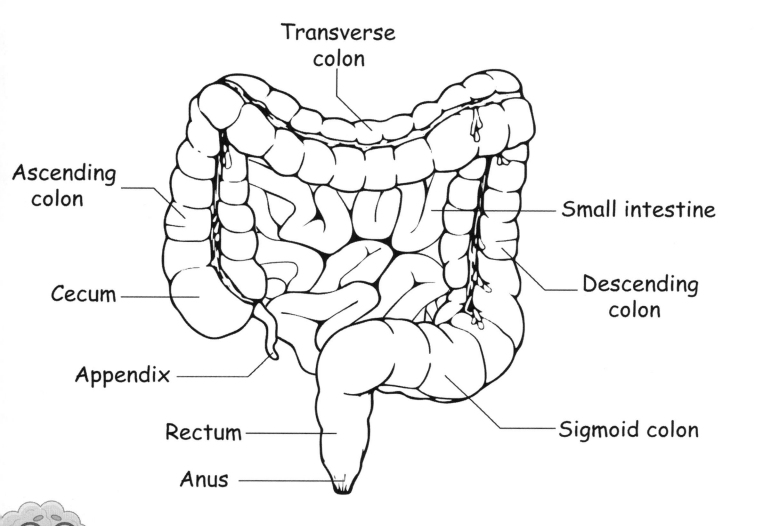

Transverse colon

Ascending colon

Small intestine

Cecum

Descending colon

Appendix

Rectum

Sigmoid colon

Anus

The intestines are the last part of the digestive system, and they are also the longest. They are long, tube-like organs that are in the abdominal cavity. They help our bodies break down the food we eat and use it.

The small and large intestines are the two parts of the human intestine.

Between the stomach and the large intestine is the small intestine. This organ takes nutrients from our food and puts them into the bloodstream. These nutrients get into our bodies and are used to do things that keep us alive.

The colon is the longest part of the large intestine, a long organ. At first, it connects to the small intestine, and at the end, it connects to the rectum. It takes in water and turns waste from food into stool, which then passes out of the body through the rectum and anus.

Pancreas

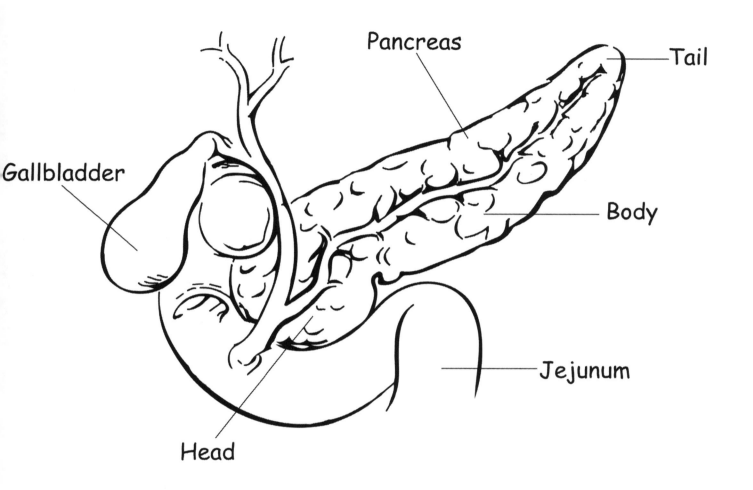

The pancreas is a gland that sits above the stomach in the upper part of the abdomen. On the surface of the pancreas, fat tissue can build up. It gives the pancreas its yellow colour and smooths the organ's surface.

The pancreas is an organ in our bodies that does two important things. First, it makes insulin, which helps check blood sugar levels. Second, it makes juices that help break down food into simpler parts like sugars, proteins, and fats for the small intestine.

Bladder

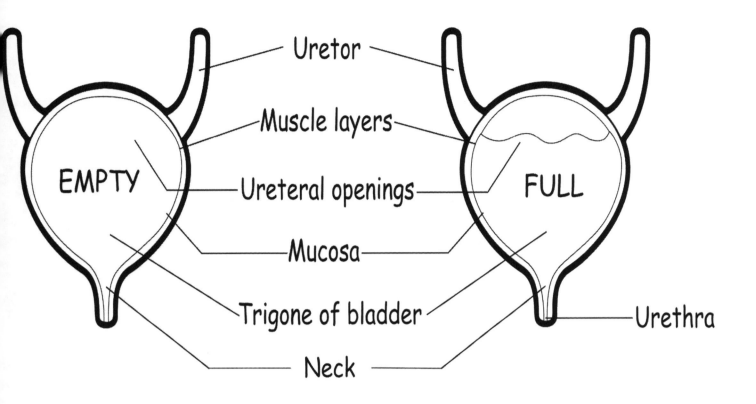

Uretor

Muscle layers

Ureteral openings

Mucosa

Trigone of bladder

Neck

EMPTY

FULL

Urethra

   The bladder is in the lower part of the abdomen and looks like a balloon. It's like a storage container for urine. As urine fills the bladder, it gets bigger, and when it's full, it tells your brain it's time to go to the bathroom. We use the muscles in our pelvic area to empty the bladder and send urine out of the body through a tube called the urethra.

   This organ looks different in men and women. It is the urethra in men and the bladder in women. Compared to men, women's bladders are smaller and sit lower.

   Men have urethras that are much longer than those of women. Also, the urethra has ducts that let sperm-filled fluid, called semen, out.

Spleen

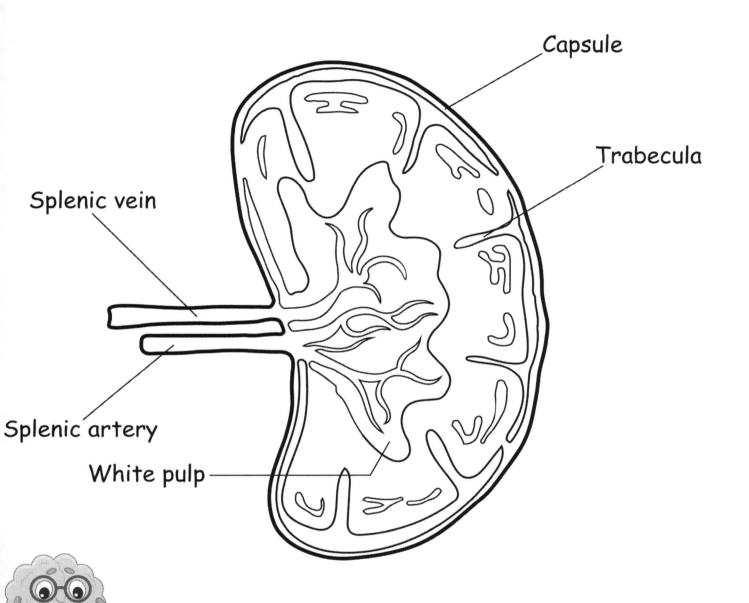

Capsule

Trabecula

Splenic vein

Splenic artery

White pulp

The spleen is an organ found on the left side of the abdomen. A healthy spleen is undetectable. Even though we can live without this organ, it is important to how our bodies work. The spleen works like a small factory that makes blood and cleans it.

It helps get rid of old and damaged red blood cells and makes new ones. It also stores white blood cells, which help fight off germs and bacteria.

II. Human organ systems and their functions

The human body is made up of many different systems that work well together to keep us alive and healthy.

To keep our systems working well, we need to take care of ourselves by eating well, getting enough exercise, and getting enough rest.

In this chapter, you'll learn how the body's systems are put together, how they work (function), and how to care for them.

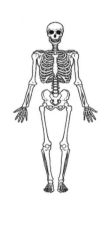

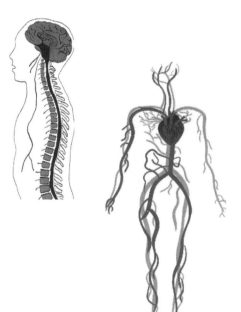

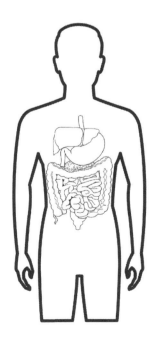

Skin

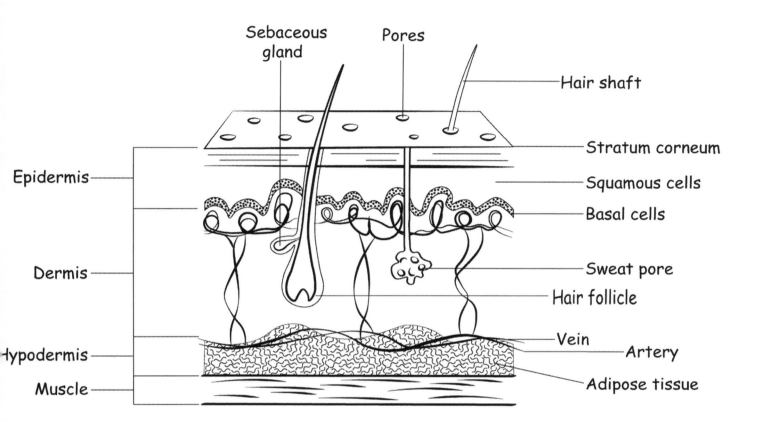

Sebaceous gland
Pores
Hair shaft
Stratum corneum
Epidermis
Squamous cells
Basal cells
Dermis
Sweat pore
Hair follicle
Hypodermis
Vein
Artery
Muscle
Adipose tissue

The skin consists of three layers:
- **Epidermis** - the top layer of skin. It protects the human body and contains melanin, the pigment that gives hair and skin their colour.
- **Dermis** - the middle layer of skin. It is strong and flexible, with sweat glands, receptors, hair roots, blood vessels, and nerves. The nerve endings in the dermis allow a person to feel things like temperature, pressure, or pain.
- **Hypodermis** - a layer of fat tissue that helps control body temperature.

Skin

Skin functions
- Protect us from outside forces (like burns, cuts, and chemicals) and dehydration.
- Secrete melanin, which gives hair and skin their colour.
- Make vitamin D3, which is important for the nervous and skeletal systems to work well.
- Sweat glands control body temperature and get rid of harmful and unnecessary substances.
- Skin receptors get information from the environment, such as touch, temperature, vibrations, pressure, etc.

How do you look after your skin?
- Skin hygiene: wash your skin daily to get rid of dust, sweat, sebum, and bacteria.
- Don't wear too-tight clothes and shoes, which can irritate and hurt the epidermis.
- Wear flip-flops to the pool to avoid getting fungal infections.
- On hot days, use sunscreen to protect your skin from UV rays that can damage it.

Locomotor system

The musculoskeletal system helps our bodies move. The human skeleton is covered by muscles, which contract and relax to make the body move.

There are two parts to the musculoskeletal system:

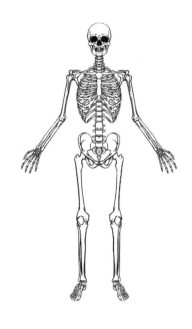

- **Passive (the skeletal system)**

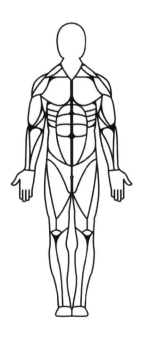

- **Active (the muscular system)**

Let's look more closely at the skeletal system.

The skeleton is made of joints and bones. About 206 bones make up an adult human body. Bones are hard organs made of protein and mineral salts. Joints are mobile bone connections that provide movement.

Skeleton

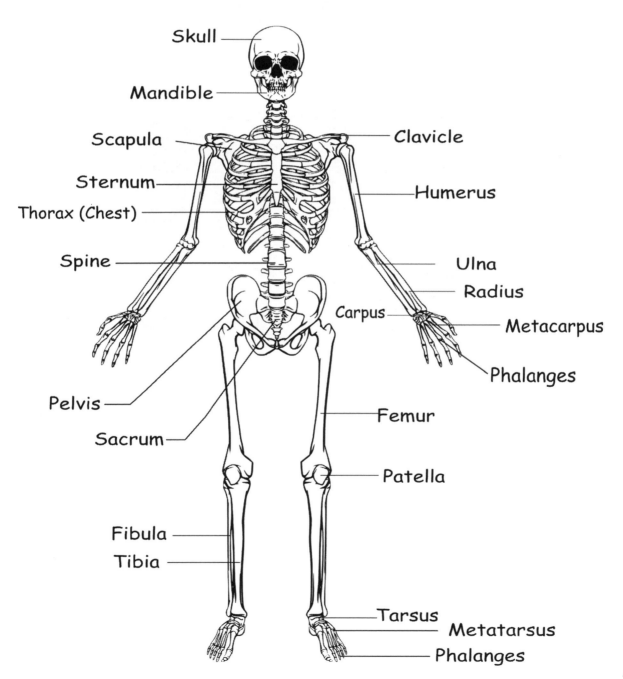

- Skull
- Mandible
- Scapula
- Sternum
- Thorax (Chest)
- Spine
- Pelvis
- Sacrum
- Fibula
- Tibia
- Clavicle
- Humerus
- Ulna
- Radius
- Carpus
- Metacarpus
- Phalanges
- Femur
- Patella
- Tarsus
- Metatarsus
- Phalanges

Skull

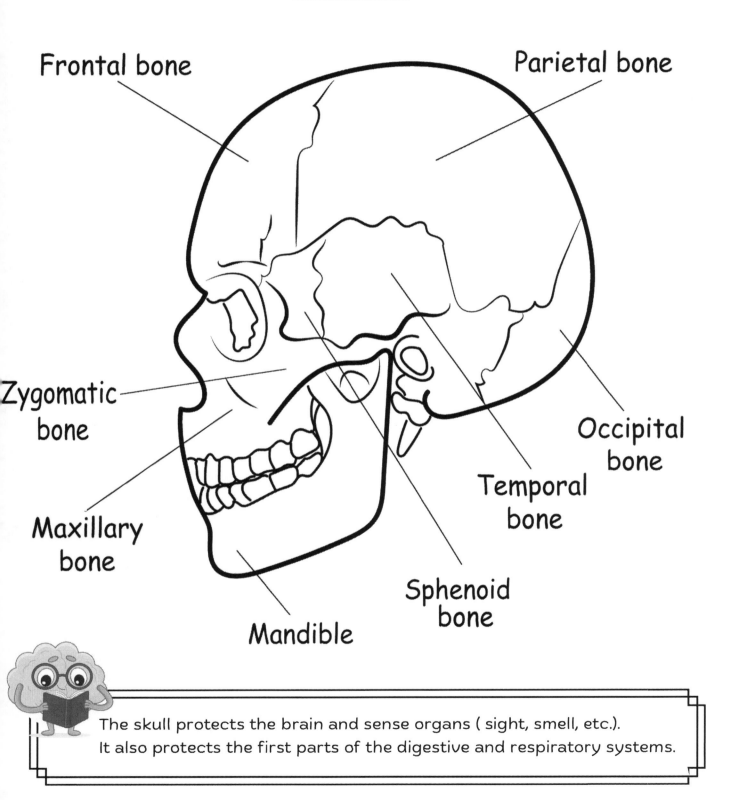

Frontal bone

Parietal bone

Zygomatic bone

Maxillary bone

Mandible

Sphenoid bone

Temporal bone

Occipital bone

The skull protects the brain and sense organs (sight, smell, etc.).
It also protects the first parts of the digestive and respiratory systems.

Chest

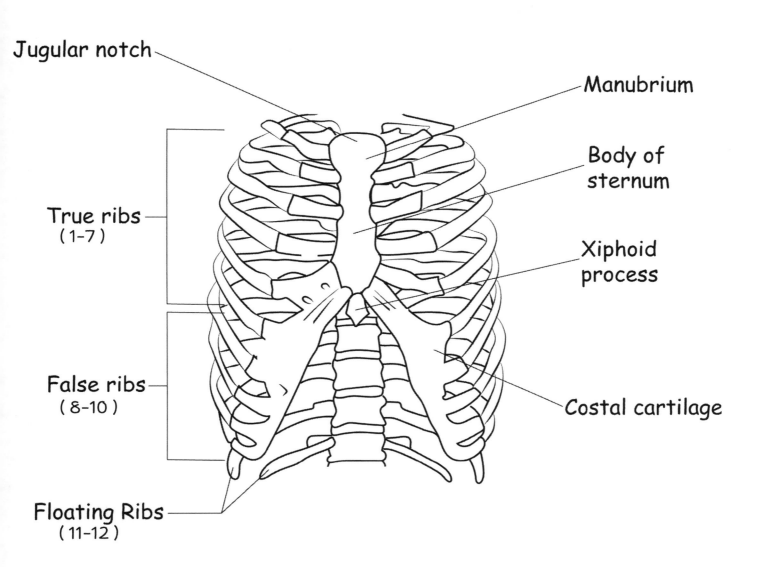

Jugular notch

Manubrium

Body of sternum

True ribs
(1-7)

Xiphoid process

False ribs
(8-10)

Costal cartilage

Floating Ribs
(11-12)

Protects our lungs and heart. Is responsible for the movements of the chest during breathing. These movements allow oxygen to be delivered to the blood and then to the entire body.

Backbone

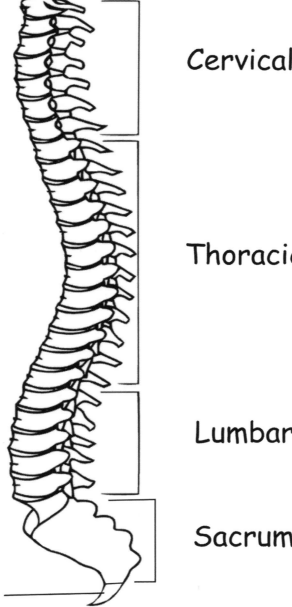

Cervical (7)

Thoracic (12)

Lumbar (5)

Sacrum (5)

Coccyx

The backbone helps keep the limbs, head, and chest bones in place. It helps us stand up straight and move our heads, necks, and upper bodies. It also keeps the important nerves that help us move safely.

Arm Bones

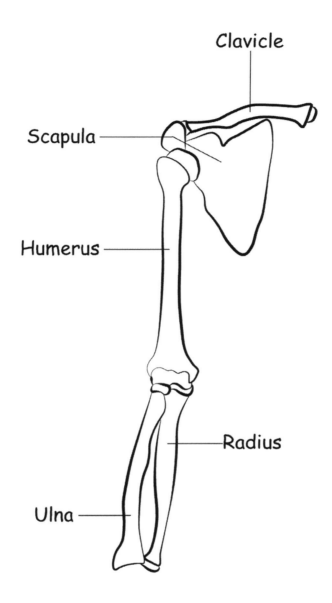

Clavicle

Scapula

Humerus

Radius

Ulna

The humerus, radius, and ulna are the bones in the arm. Their job is to support and move the upper arm and hand.

The humerus connects the shoulder to the elbow. The radius and ulna connect the elbow to the wrist. Together, they allow for a wide range of motion, including flexion, extension, and rotation.

Leg Bones

Upper leg bone

Lower leg bones

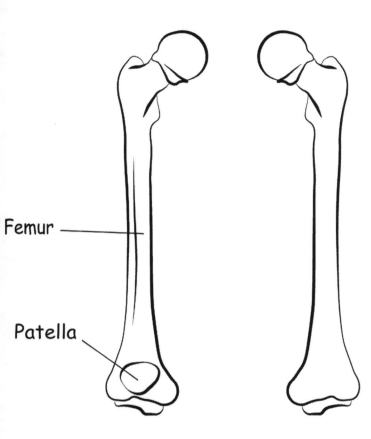

Femur

Patella

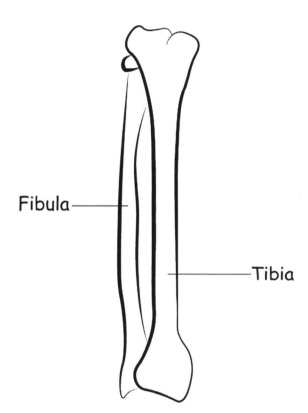

Fibula

Tibia

The bones in the legs, especially the femur, tibia, and fibula, help support and move the lower body, allowing us to walk, run, jump, and stand.

The femur, the largest bone in the body, connects the hip to the knee and carries most of the lower body's weight. The tibia and fibula connect the knee to the ankle, keeping the leg stable.

Pelvic Girdle

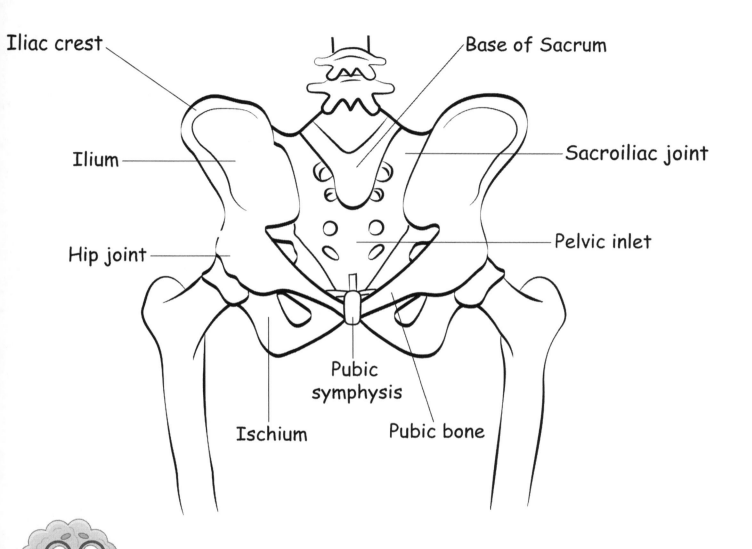

Iliac crest

Base of Sacrum

Ilium

Sacroiliac joint

Hip joint

Pelvic inlet

Pubic symphysis

Ischium

Pubic bone

The pelvic girdle helps transfer the upper body's weight to the legs, which lets us stand and move. It also protects the organs in the lower abdomen and pelvis, such as the bladder, rectum, and reproductive organs.

It gives the legs and spine a stable base, which is important for walking, running, and jumping. The female pelvis is wider and rounder than the male pelvis, where babies are born.

Knee

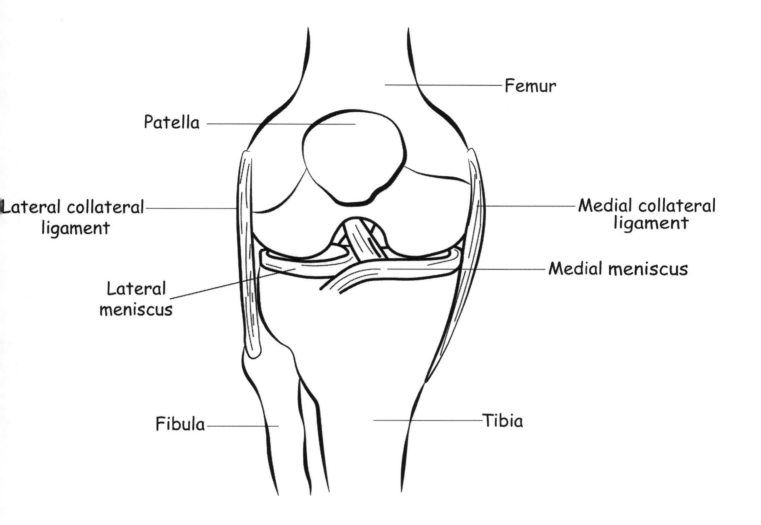

Patella

Femur

Lateral collateral ligament

Medial collateral ligament

Lateral meniscus

Medial meniscus

Fibula

Tibia

The knee is the joint where the tibia and femur meet. It's like the hinge on a door, letting the leg bend and straighten. It helps you walk, run, jump, and do other things like playing sports or climbing stairs.

Your knee also has a small bone on the outside called the fibula that helps keep you stable. It's surrounded by muscles and tendons that help move the knee in different directions. It's also a shock absorber, which helps reduce the impact when you jump or run, keeping your leg safe and healthy.

 Let's learn more about the muscular system.

The muscular system is made up of three types of muscles:
- **Skeletal muscles** (also called striated muscles) depend on our willpower to move and change the body's position (like when dancing).
- **Smooth muscles** do not depend on our willpower and are found on the surface of organs like the bladder, bronchi, uterus, GI tract, and blood vessels.
- **Cardiac muscle** does not depend on our willpower and pumps blood through the heart, which then circulates throughout the body.

Muscular System

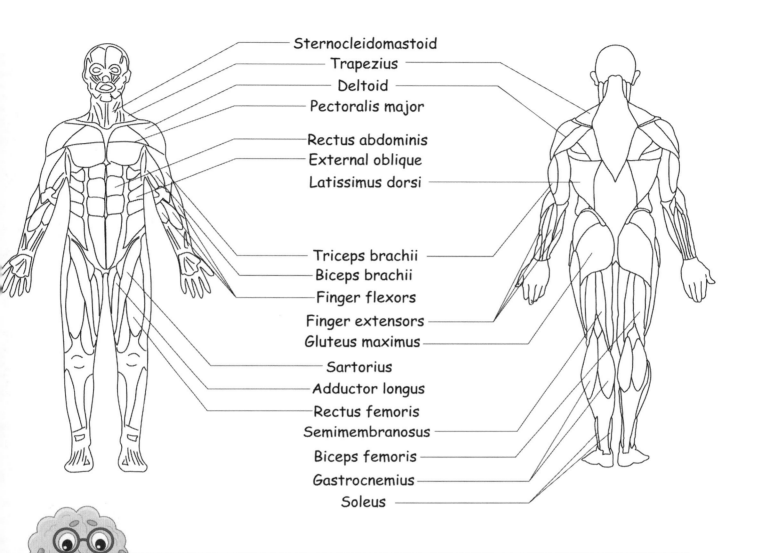

Sternocleidomastoid
Trapezius
Deltoid
Pectoralis major
Rectus abdominis
External oblique
Latissimus dorsi

Triceps brachii
Biceps brachii
Finger flexors
Finger extensors
Gluteus maximus
Sartorius
Adductor longus
Rectus femoris
Semimembranosus
Biceps femoris
Gastrocnemius
Soleus

Skeletal muscles and what they do:
- **Head muscles** allow the tongue, jaw, mandible, and eyeballs to move and affect facial expressions.
- **Neck muscles** allow the head to move, twist, bend, and tilt.
- **Chest muscles** allow the upper limbs to move and are responsible for the descent of the ribs when you inhale and exhale.
- **Abdominal muscles** help you breathe and allow the body to straighten, bend, rotate, and stay balanced.
- **Back muscles** keep the body stable and allow the ribs, shoulders, and shoulder blades to move.
- **Upper and lower limb muscles** move the limbs.

Locomotor system

Functions of the locomotor system

Skeletal system	The muscular system
• Gives the body its shape. • Determines its length. • Protects the organs inside the body. • Keeps the body standing up straight. • Stores calcium and phosphorus.	• It moves the body. • Keeps the organs in place. • Models the body's shape.

How do you take care of your locomotor system?
- Load your spine evenly (carry your rucksack on both shoulders).
- Exercise regularly.
- Wear comfortable shoes.
- Eat foods high in vitamin D, calcium, and phosphorus.

Digestive system

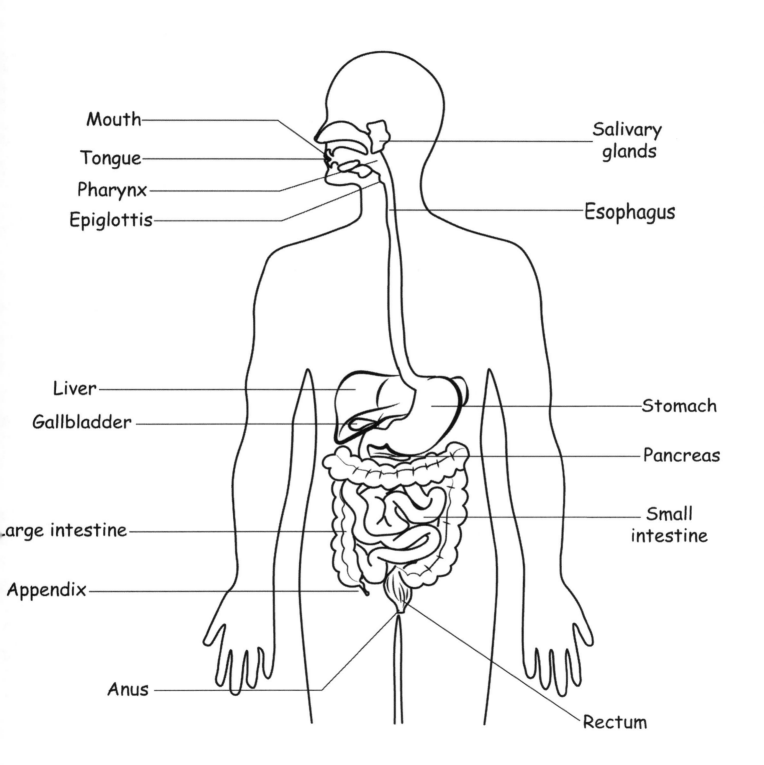

Mouth

Tongue

Pharynx

Epiglottis

Salivary glands

Esophagus

Liver

Gallbladder

Stomach

Pancreas

Large intestine

Small intestine

Appendix

Anus

Rectum

33

Digestive system

The digestive system's organs and their roles:

a) Digestive tract:
- **Oral cavity** - where the teeth break up food, mix it with saliva and then clump it together.
- **Esophagus** - moves food from your mouth to your stomach.
- **Stomach** - the digestion process begins.
- **Small intestine** - digestion continues, and food particles are absorbed into the blood.
- **Large intestine** - water is absorbed; undigested food becomes faeces, then is passed out of the body through the anus.

b) Digestive glands
- **Salivary glands** - make saliva, which softens food and helps partially digest it.
- **Liver** - produces bile for the small intestine; this bile breaks down fat into droplets, which makes it easier for digestive substances to break down fat.
- **Pancreas** - substances for the small intestine that break down proteins, sugars, and fats.

Functions of the digestive system
Its job is to get, break down, and digest food. The remains of undigested food are excreted from the body through the anus in the form of feces.

How should the digestive system be taken care of?
- Eat regularly.
- Chew your food well.
- Eat fruits and vegetables or bread with large grains.
- Wash your hands before eating.

Respiratory system

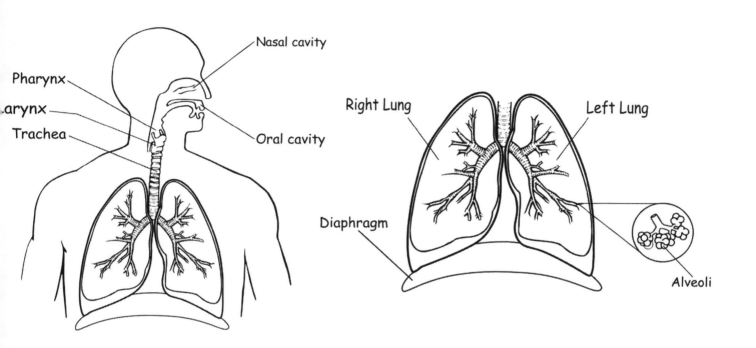

Pharynx
Larynx
Trachea
Nasal cavity
Oral cavity

Right Lung
Left Lung
Diaphragm
Alveoli

<u>The organs of the respiratory system and their roles:</u>

a) Airways

- **Nasal cavity** - in charge of moistening, warming, and cleaning the air we breathe in (inhale).
- **Larynx** - where the vocal cords vibrate and make sounds when we breathe out (exhale).
- **Trachea and bronchi** - where the air is cleaned and sent to the lungs.

b) The Lungs

The lungs are where gas exchange happens. Oxygen goes into the body, and carbon dioxide goes out.

Inhalation and exhalation

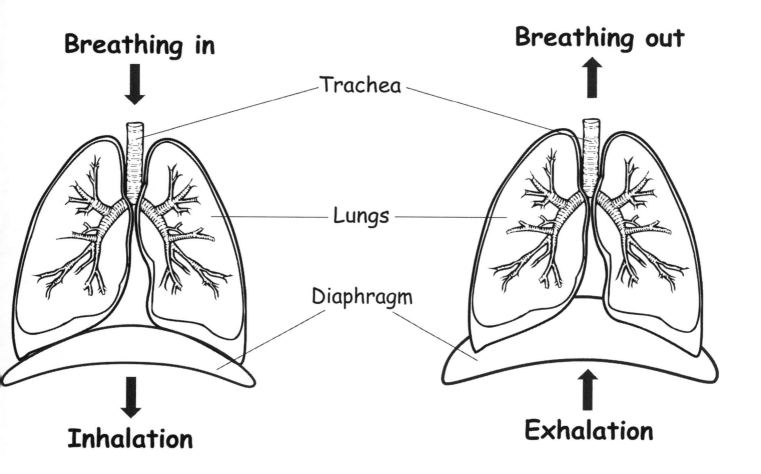

Breathing in

Trachea

Lungs

Diaphragm

Breathing out

Inhalation

Exhalation

This is possible because the chest moves in a steady rhythm. These movements allow the intercostal muscles and the diaphragm to contract and relax.

Respiratory system

Differences between inhalation and exhalation

	Inhalation	Exhalation
Phase	Active (the muscles actively contract when the air goes into the lungs)	Passive (the muscles relax when the air is pushed out of the lungs)
Intercostal muscles and diaphragm	Contracts	Expands
Chest	Rises and volume increases	Collapses and decreases in volume
Alveolar pressure	Decreases	Increases
Air	Reaches the lungs	Exit the lungs

Functions of the respiratory system

The respiratory system's main job is to exchange gases. It takes oxygen from the air, which goes to the lungs and gets rid of harmful waste products from metabolism, like carbon dioxide.

How do you take care of your respiratory system?

- By doing aerobic activities like biking, swimming, running, and walking.
- Avoiding smoking, vaping, and breathing in secondhand smoke.
- Limiting fat, especially animal fats, sugar, and salt in your diet.
- Adding garlic, green tea, honey, and herbs (thyme, ginger, turmeric) to your diet to strengthen your immune system.
- Washing your hands thoroughly and regularly.
- Keep a safe distance from people who are sneezing and coughing to keep yourself and other people from getting sick.

Circulatory system

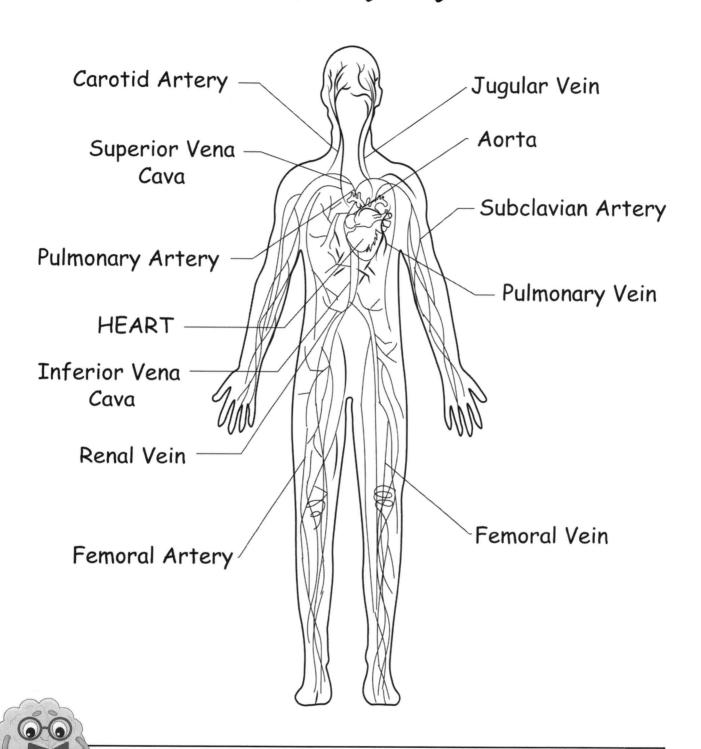

Carotid Artery

Superior Vena Cava

Pulmonary Artery

HEART

Inferior Vena Cava

Renal Vein

Femoral Artery

Jugular Vein

Aorta

Subclavian Artery

Pulmonary Vein

Femoral Vein

The circulatory system is called a "closed system" because the blood doesn't flow into the body's empty spaces. Instead, blood flows through the blood vessels (veins and arteries).

Circulatory system

The organs of the circulatory system and their roles:
a) Heart
- By contracting and relaxing, the heart makes sure that blood flows quickly through the blood vessels.

b) Blood vessels:
- **Arteries** – blood vessels that carry blood from the heart to the rest of the body; they have thick, elastic walls; blood has high pressure and flows quickly; the AORTA is the largest artery in the body.
- **Veins** – blood vessels that carry blood back to the heart; they have thin walls; blood has low pressure and flows slowly.
- **Capillaries** – the smallest blood vessels with thin walls. They connect to every cell in the body and bring oxygen and food to the cells.

Functions of the circulatory system
- The circulatory system helps keep the chemical balance in our bodies so that our organs and tissues can work properly. The blood carries oxygen and nutrients to all of our organs and tissues.
- It also removes harmful substances and wastes from our bodies.
- Blood also helps control our body temperature by bringing heat to places where it is cold and taking heat away from places that are too hot.

How to take care of your circulatory system?
- Eat healthy food: try to eat a lot of fruits and vegetables and stay away from too much candy, fats, and salt.
- Drink enough water: water is very important for your body because it keeps you hydrated and removes toxins.
- Regularly exercise.
- Don't smoke cigarettes.

Nervous system

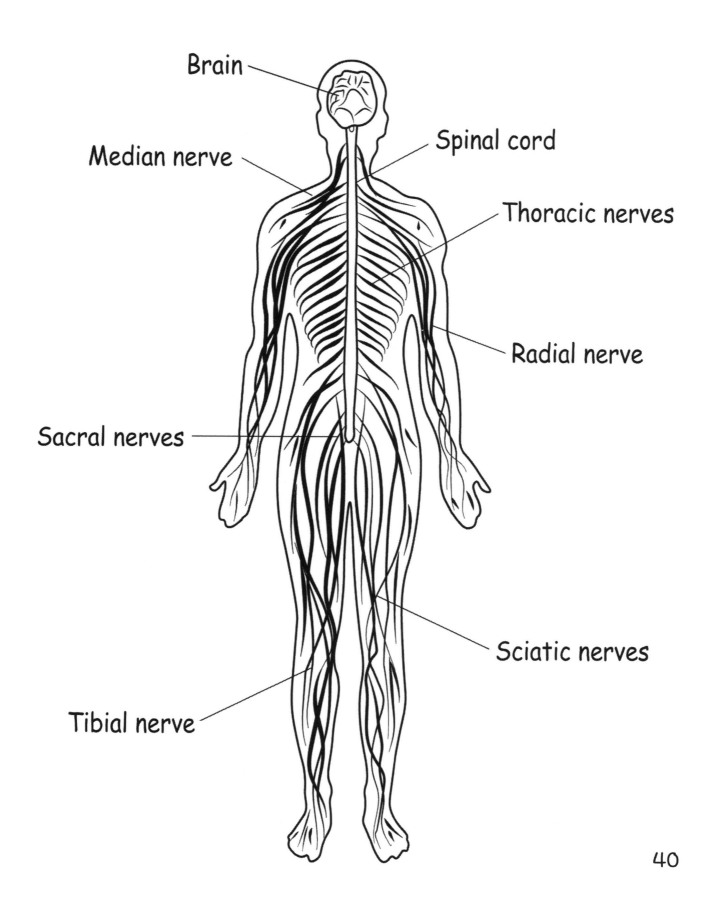

Brain

Spinal cord

Median nerve

Thoracic nerves

Radial nerve

Sacral nerves

Sciatic nerves

Tibial nerve

Nervous system

Organs of the nervous system and their roles:

The nervous system is divided into:

I. Central nervous system

a) **Brain** - takes in and processes information directly from the outside and inside world. The parts of the brain are:

- **The brain** - is in charge of thinking, planning, and reasoning, as well as the senses of touch, sight, and hearing.
- **The brainstem** - the part of the brain that sends messages to the rest of the body. It controls important things like breathing and heartbeat. It also helps us stay awake and alert.
- **The cerebellum** - is in charge of keeping the body in balance. It controls every body movement, so we can stand and walk straight.

b) **The spinal cord** - is like a long cable that connects the brain to the rest of the body. It helps the brain send messages to the muscles and skin so that we can move and feel. The spinal cord also helps us act quickly, like pulling our hands away from something hot when we touch it.

II. Peripheral nervous system

- **Cranial (brain) nerves** - 12 pairs - come out of the brain and help us see, hear, smell, speak, and taste. They are arranged around the skull and send messages from the brain to different body parts.
- **Spinal nerves** - 31 pairs - come out of the spinal cord and control our movements, sense pain and temperature, and send signals from the brain to our limbs and other body parts.

Nervous system

Remember!!!

A neuron (nerve cell) is the main component of the nervous system. It is a small cell in the brain and body that helps us think and move. Its job is to get messages from other neurons and send them to different body parts. Think of it as a telephone operator that connects calls!

Neuron

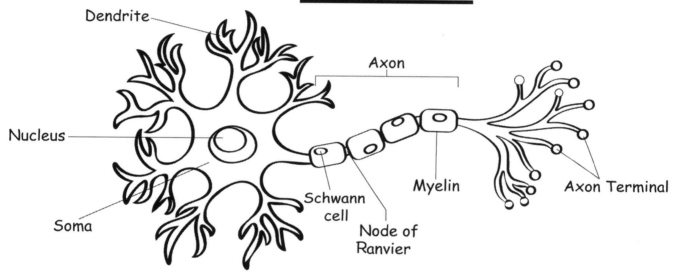

Soma - controls and directs the cell's activities.

Dendrites - receive messages from other cells and return them to the cell.

The nucleus - is like the cell's "control centre". DNA, made up of genetic material, is found in the nucleus. DNA is like a set of instructions for the cell. It tells the cell how to grow and what it should do.

Axon - sends messages to other cells.

Schwann cells - help send messages through the axon faster and farther away from each other.

The nodes of Ranvier - allow messages to jump quickly from one part of the axon to another.

Myelin - a special coating on the axon that helps messages move quickly.

Axon terminals - use chemicals called neurotransmitters to send messages to other cells.

Nervous system

Functions of the nervous system

- Receives and analyses information coming from the sense organs (touch, hearing, sight or taste).
- Monitors how our internal organs are working.
- Responsible for memory and intelligence.
- Controls the body's actions, including those that are conscious (muscle movement) and unconscious (breathing, sneezing, etc.).

How to take care of your nervous system?

- Get at least 8 hours of sleep each night.
- When reading, turn on the light.
- Wash your ears.
- On sunny days, wear sunglasses.
- Avoid excessive noise and listening to loud music through headphones.

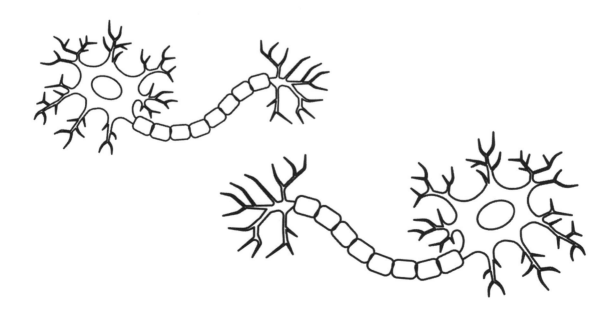

Excretory system

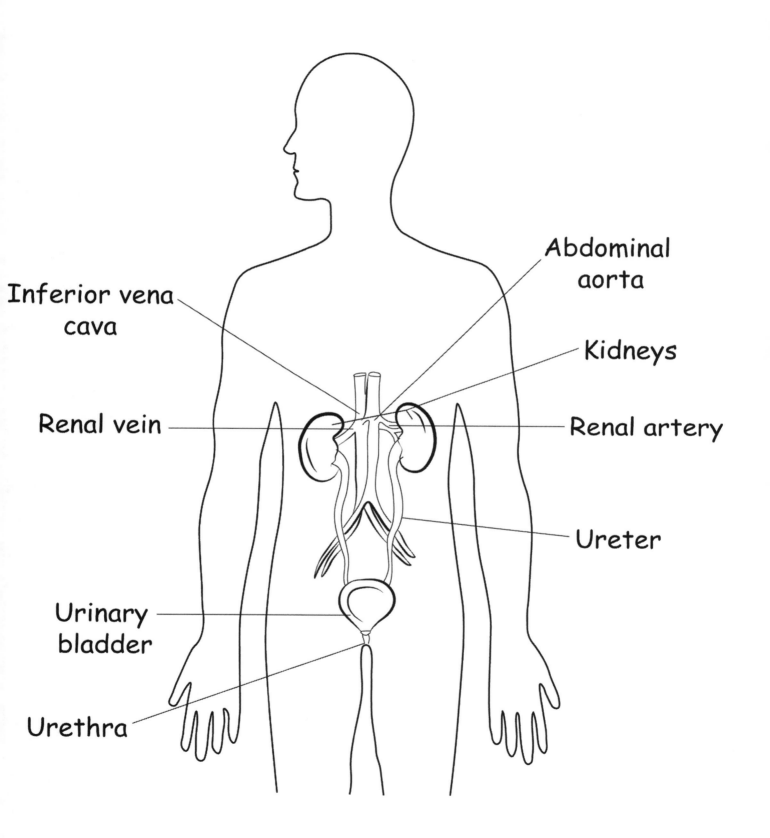

Inferior vena cava

Abdominal aorta

Kidneys

Renal vein

Renal artery

Ureter

Urinary bladder

Urethra

Excretory system

The excretory system's organs and their roles:

a) **The two kidneys** make urine and clean the blood of unwanted or harmful substances.

b) The pathways that drain urine, which include:

- **The two ureters** - carry urine from the kidneys to the bladder.
- **The bladder** - temporarily stores urine that flows out of the kidneys through the ureters.
- **The urethra** - carries urine out of the body.

Functions of the excretory system

- In charge of getting rid of waste products like uric acid and urea.
- Controls the amount of water and mineral salts in the body so that their levels are almost always the same.

How to take care of your excretory system?

- Don't hold your urine for too long.
- Make sure to drink enough water, which helps keep your excretory system in good shape and makes it easier to get rid of toxins.
- Don't eat too much salt because it can make you retain water and mess up your electrolytes.
- To avoid infection, use intimate hygiene lotion when you wash your area.
- Avoid dirty places that are likely to make you sick, like public toilets and swimming pools.
- Don't sit on the cold ground.
- Dress warmly when it's cold to avoid getting a cold in your kidneys or bladder.

Reproductive system

Humans' reproductive system – a new organism is made when an ovum (female reproductive cell) joins with a sperm (male reproductive cell).

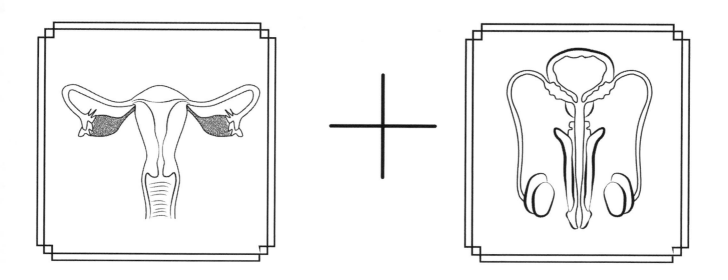

Female reproductive system

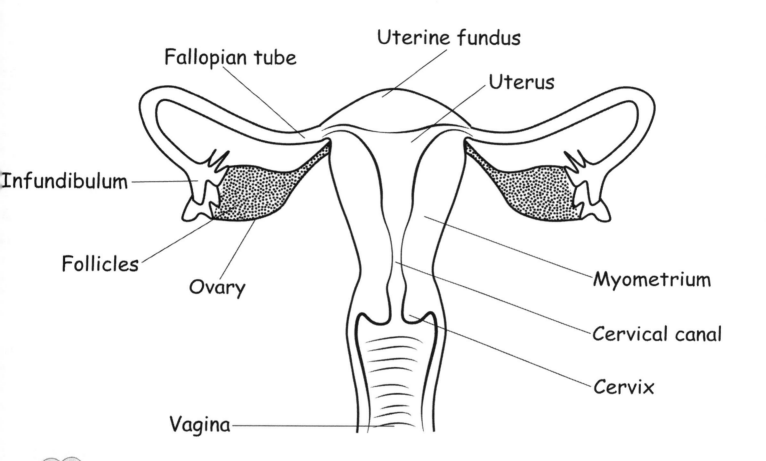

Fallopian tube

Uterine fundus

Uterus

Infundibulum

Follicles

Ovary

Myometrium

Cervical canal

Cervix

Vagina

The organs that make up the female reproductive system and how they work:

- **Two ovaries** – produce female reproductive cells called ova.
- **Two fallopian tubes** – where the egg and sperm meet.
- **Uterus** – where the embryo grows.
- **The vagina** – where the baby comes out during birth and where menstrual blood comes out (during menstruation).

Male reproductive system

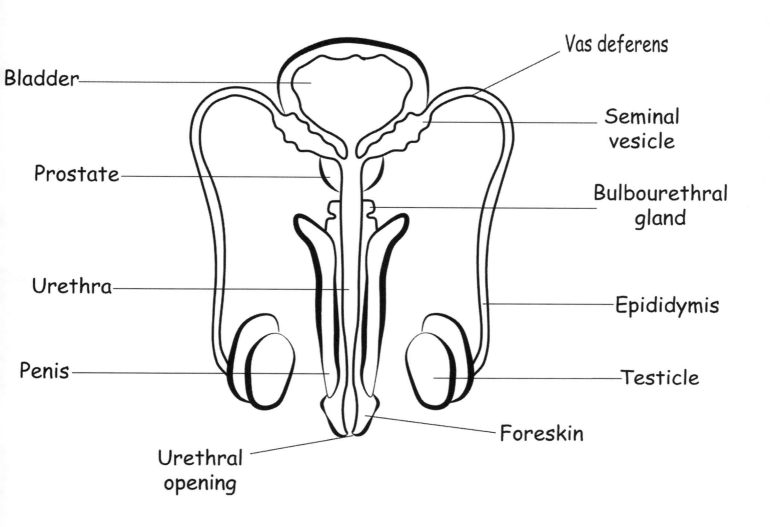

Bladder

Prostate

Urethra

Penis

Vas deferens

Seminal vesicle

Bulbourethral gland

Epididymis

Testicle

Foreskin

Urethral opening

The male reproductive system's organs and what they do:
- **Two testicles** - produce male reproductive cells called sperm cells.
- **Two vas deferens** - where sperm cells travel from the testes to the urethra.
- **The penis** (male member) - where sperm (the fluid that contains sperm cells) comes out.

Reproductive system

Functions of the reproductive system

The reproductive system's function is to bring offspring into the world and maintain the continuity of the species. Through fertilisation (joining of the reproductive cells: egg and sperm), a new organism is created.

How to take care of your reproductive system?

- Take care of your intimate hygiene by washing your genitalia well every day. If you don't have access to water, like when camping, you can use special wipes to clean your genitalia.
- Stay active. Physical activity and a healthy diet strengthen your immune system, keeping you from getting sick.
- Wear underwear that is clean and comfortable. Underwear that is too tight can hurt your genitourinary system.
- Change out of your wet swimsuit as soon as possible and put on a clean, dry one to prevent bacteria from growing and avoid infections in the intimate area.
- Use a disposable toilet seat cover when using a public toilet.

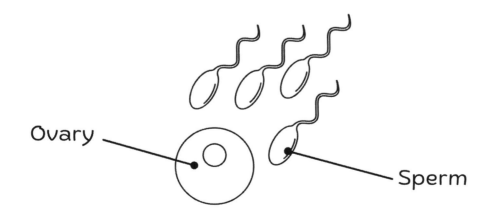

Endocrine system

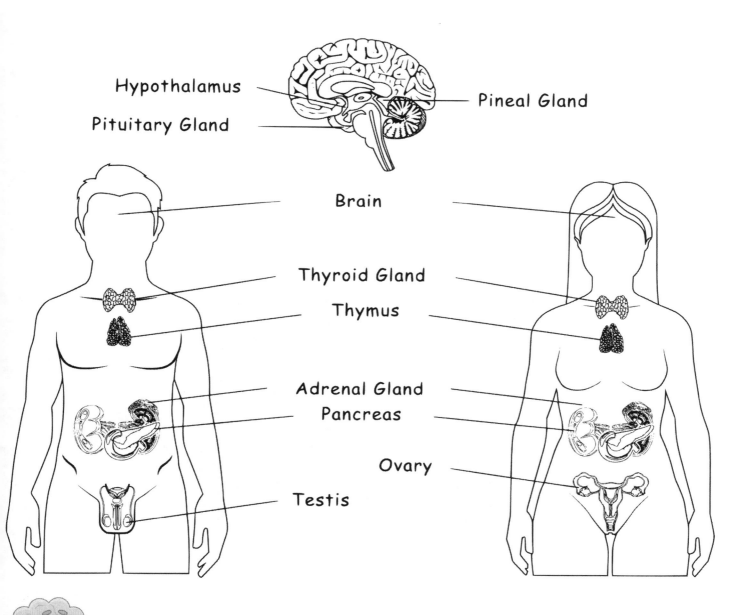

Hypothalamus

Pituitary Gland

Pineal Gland

Brain

Thyroid Gland

Thymus

Adrenal Gland

Pancreas

Ovary

Testis

The endocrine system is made up of organs that make hormones, which are chemicals that help the body do many things. These hormones get to different parts of the body through the bloodstream. They help control things like growth, mood, and energy levels.

Endocrine glands, found in different parts of the body, are very important to how this system works.

Endocrine system

The endocrine glands include:

- **Pituitary gland** - makes hormones that control other glands in the body and keep growth and development in check.
- **Hypothalamus** - helps to control things like hunger, thirst, and body temperature. It also makes hormones that control the pituitary gland.
- **Pineal gland** - makes the hormone melatonin, which helps control when you sleep and when you wake up.
- **Thyroid gland** - makes hormones that control the body's metabolism and affect how people grow and develop.
- **Parathyroid glands** - make hormones that control the amount of calcium in the body.
- **Thymus gland** - makes hormones that help the immune system fight off infections.
- **Adrenal glands** - make hormones that help the body deal with stress, control blood sugar levels, and regulate blood pressure.
- **Pancreas** - makes hormones that control how much sugar is in the blood and enzymes that help break down food.
- **Testes** (in men) - make and release sperm, which is used for reproduction.
- **Ovaries** (in women)- make and release eggs, which are used for reproduction. They also control the menstrual cycle and pregnancy.

Functions of the endocrine system

The endocrine system makes hormones that send messages to different body parts through the bloodstream. These hormones help control important things like growth, metabolism, reproduction, and how we react to stress. The endocrine system keeps everything in our bodies in check.

How to care for the endocrine system?

- Eat protein-rich foods like fish, meat, and eggs.
- Exercise every day.
- Don't add too much sugar to your meals (to avoid becoming overweight or getting diabetes).
- Manage your stress by listening to relaxing music, doing yoga, getting a massage, or meditating.

Sense organs

There are 5 basic senses:
- Sight
- Hearing
- Smell
- Taste
- Touch

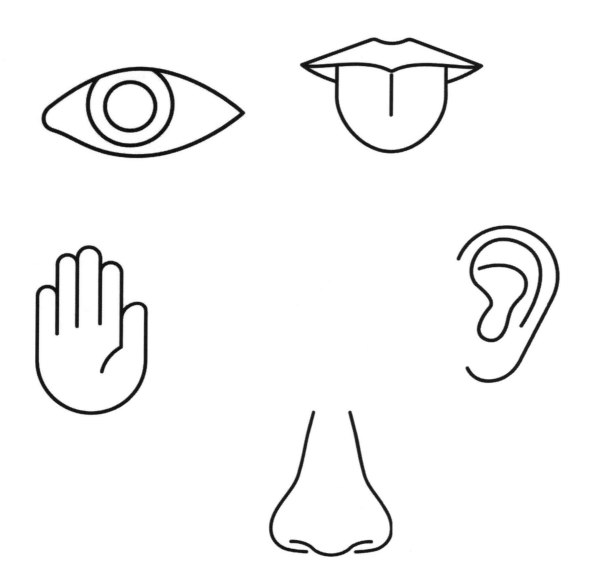

Sight

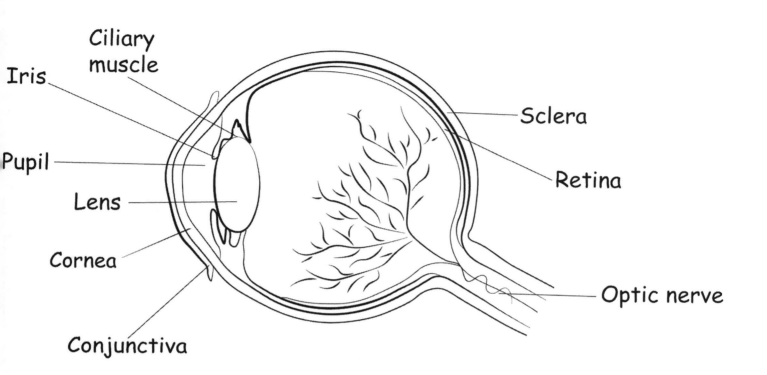

Iris

Ciliary muscle

Pupil

Lens

Cornea

Conjunctiva

Sclera

Retina

Optic nerve

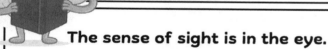

The sense of sight is in the eye.

It lets you tell the difference between colours and see things. Through the pupil, the light gets into the eye. Then, with the lens's help, it focuses on the retina. Light signals are turned into nerve impulses and sent to the brain. The image is shrunk and turned around on the retina. The proximity of the eyes to the front of the head makes it possible to see in three dimensions.

How do you take care of your sight?

- Take breaks when you're looking at screens for a long time.
- Turn on the light when you read a book or write.
- Don't smoke and stay away from secondhand smoke.
- Wear sunglasses outside to keep the sun's UV rays from hurting your eyes.

Hearing

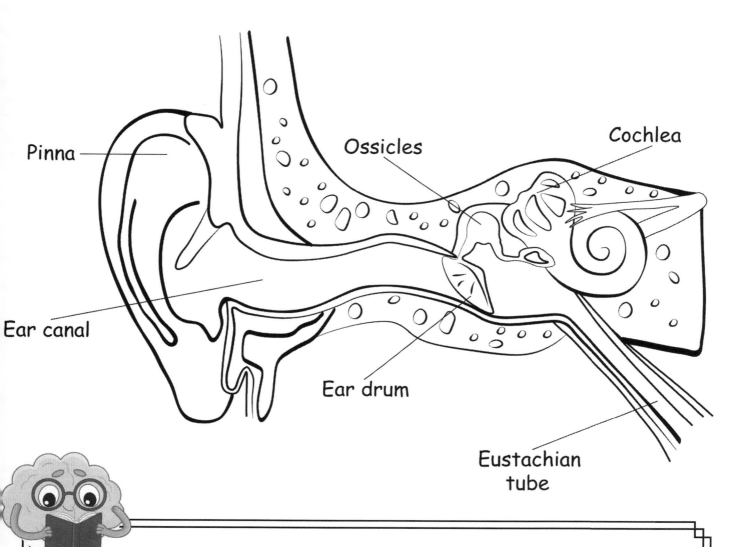

Pinna

Ossicles

Cochlea

Ear canal

Ear drum

Eustachian tube

The sense of hearing is in the ear.

The part of the ear that sticks out looks like a shell. This is because sound travels through the outer part of the ear and into the inner part as vibrations. The sound waves then go deep into the ear and brain. Then, the brain figures out what the sound is.

How do I take care of my hearing?

- Don't use an ear stick to clean your ears.
- Wear a hat on cold days.
- Don't listen to loud music, especially with headphones.
- Use air conditioning sensibly.

Smell

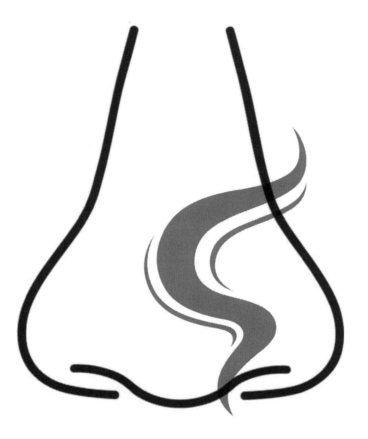

The sense of smell is in the nose.

Thanks to our sense of smell, we can tell the difference between odours in the air. This sense warns us of danger, such as gas leaks. Also, our sense of smell quickly goes away, so we can't smell after a while.

How do I look after my sense of smell (olfactory system)?

- Avoid foul smells like tobacco smoke, chemicals, and others that may irritate your system.
- Eat zinc-rich foods like lean meat or fish.
- Use a humidifier at home because moist air helps the membranes in your nose stay moist.
- Clean your nose often so you won't clog your nasal passages, and your sense of smell will stay clear.

Taste

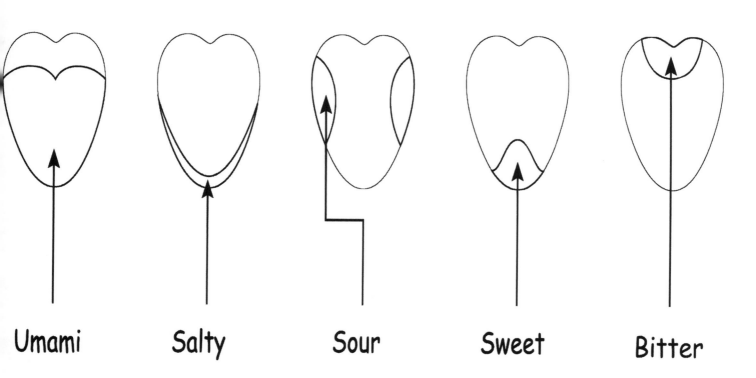

Umami   Salty   Sour   Sweet   Bitter

The sense of taste is in the tongue.

It finds information about the substances contained in food. It helps us decide if food is tasty, fresh, and safe. We say that something is sweet, salty, sour, or bitter. Taste lets us know when food isn't fresh or safe to eat. The senses of taste and smell are connected. For example, it's hard to taste food if you have a runny nose.

How do I take care of my sense of taste?

- Brush your tongue and teeth.
- Chew gum to clean your mouth and speed up digestion so that you can taste things better.
- Don't eat too many spicy or hot foods because they hurt your taste buds.

Touch

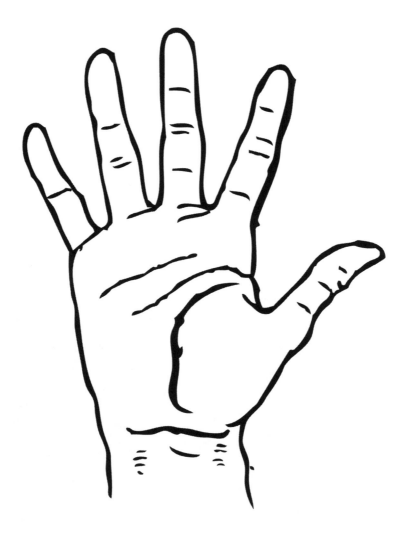

The sense of touch is in the skin.

It receives information about the force of touch, pressure or pain, and the temperature of the environment. In addition, the skin on the lips and fingertips is very sensitive.

How to take care of your sense of touch?

- Avoid skin diseases like burns, bites, and allergic reactions.
- Wear clothes that fit well and aren't too tight or rough.
- Wash and moisturise your skin every day to keep it clean.
- Regular exercise, like yoga or massage, keeps the skin soft.
- Stress can make you sweat a lot and make your skin dry.

57

III. Knowledge test

Task 1.

The human organs are shown below:

a) Colour the organs and give their names

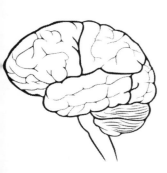 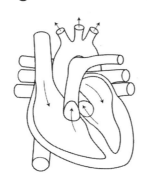 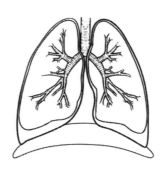 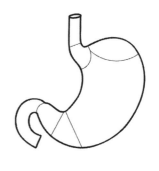

....

b) Match the human organs above with the names of the systems listed below:

• Digestive system –
• Nervous system –
• Circulatory system –
• Respiratory system –

c) Name one function of each of the following systems:

• Digestive system –

• Nervous system –

• Circulatory system –

• Respiratory system –

Task 2.

Colour the organs that are part of the digestive system.

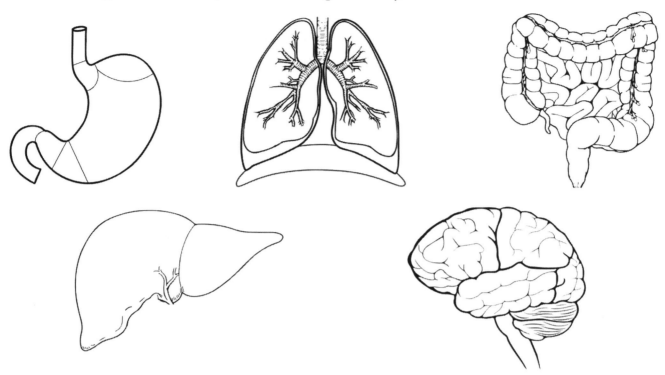

Task 3.

A human skeleton is depicted below.

a) Colour and label the following parts of the skeleton:

- Skull
- Chest
- Spine

b) State the functions of the following:

- Skull –

- Chest –

- Spine –

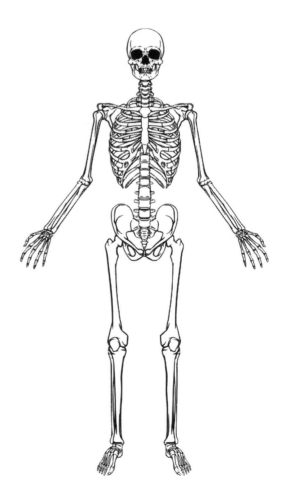

Task 4.

The following organs are listed below.

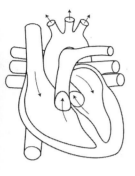 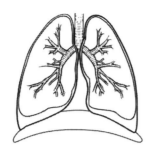 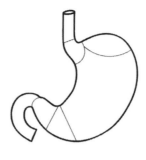 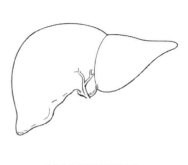

....

a) Name the organs

b) Colour the organ where gas exchange takes place, and write the name of its system

Name of the system: ....

Task 5.

Colour the organ below:

a) Give its name

....

b) Mark the right and left ventricle and the right and left atrium.

c) What system does this organ build (give its name), and what does it consist of?

Name of system:

....

The system includes:

....

d) The difference between arteries and veins:

• arteries –

• veins –

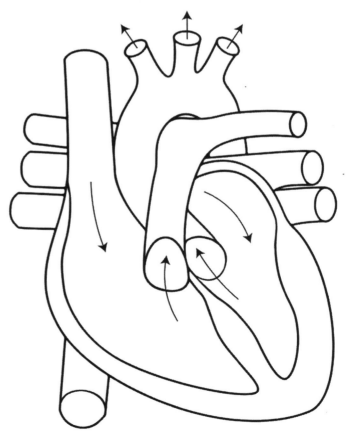

60

Task 6

Match the following organ names with the reproductive system:

Urethra, Testicle, Penis, Ovary, Uterus, Prostate, Vagina, Fallopian Tube

female reproductive system

male reproductive system

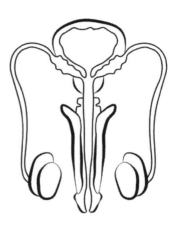

. . . .

Task 7.

The main sense organs are listed below.

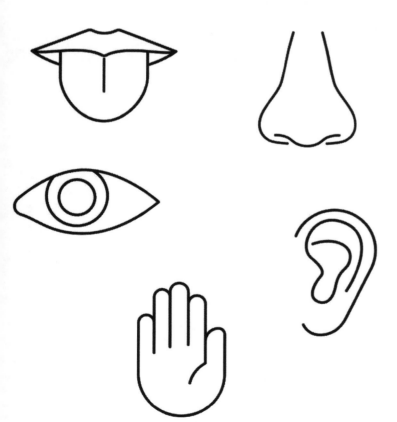

a) Colour the sense organs and name them;

b) Match where each sense organ is located:

- Skin –
- Tongue –
- Eye –
- Ear –
- Nose –

61

Task 8.

Write what the human system is and name the organs

Name of the system: ....

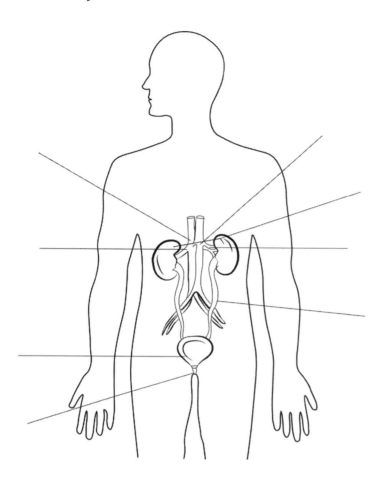

Task 9.

The nervous system is shown below.

a) Colour the brain and spinal cord;
b) Write the name of the nerve cells
in the nervous system

....

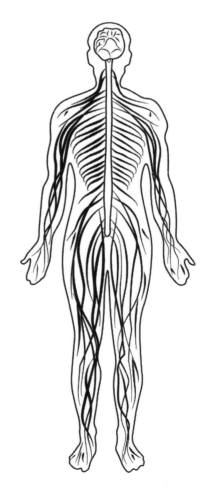

Task 10.

Point to the thyroid gland in the diagram and colour it in.

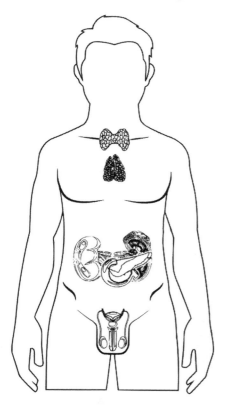 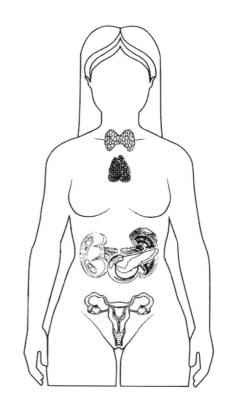

What role does the thyroid gland play in the body?

....

Task 11.

The drawing shows human skin.

a) Locate the sweat pore and colour it in.

b) Give two functions of the skin:

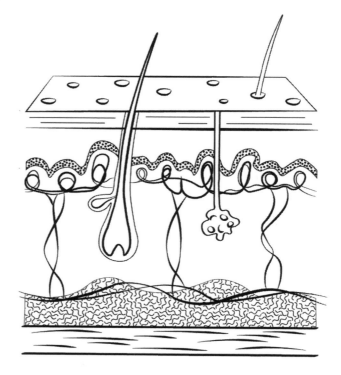

1.

2.

Answers to the test

Task 1.

a)

 Brain, Heart, Lungs, Stomach

b)

Digestive system - stomach

Nervous system - brain

Circulatory system - heart

Respiratory system - lungs

c)

Digestive system

Takes in food, breaks it down, digests it (with the help of digestive enzymes), and absorbs it, getting rid of any leftover food.

Nervous system

Receives and analyses information from the sense organs (touch, hearing, sight or taste).

Circulatory system

Circulating blood delivers oxygen and nutrients to all of our organs and tissues. Also, it gets rid of harmful things from our bodies.

Respiratory system

GIt gets oxygen from the outside and gets rid of carbon dioxide from the inside.

Task 2.

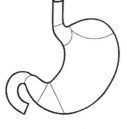

Stomach

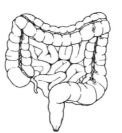

Intestines

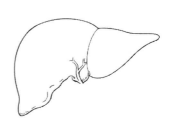

Liver

Task 3.

a)

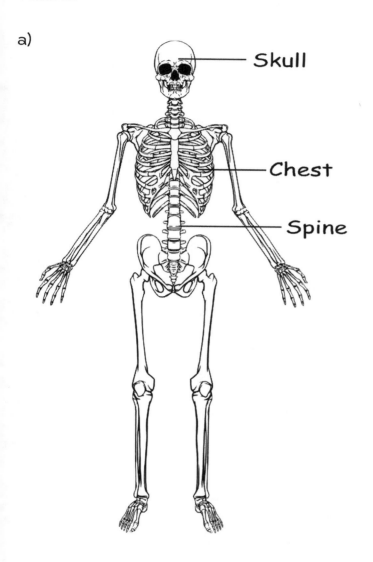

Skull

Chest

Spine

b)

Skull – protects the sense organs and the brain; it also protects the first parts of the respiratory and digestive systems

Chest – protects the lungs and heart

Spine – supports the skeleton of the limbs, skull and chest

Task 4.

a)

Heart, Lungs, Stomach, Liver

b)

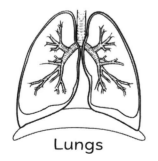

Lungs

Name of system: the respiratory system.

Task 5.

a)

Heart

b)

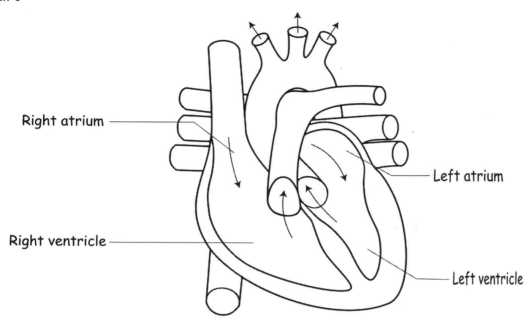

Right atrium

Left atrium

Right ventricle

Left ventricle

c)

Name of the system: the circulatory system.

The system includes the heart and blood vessels.

d)

Arteries - blood vessels that carry blood from the heart to the rest of the body; they have thick, elastic walls; blood has high pressure and flows quickly; the AORTA is the largest artery in the body

Veins - blood vessels that carry blood back to the heart; they have thin walls; blood has low pressure and flows slowly.

Task 6.

Female reproductive system:

Ovary, Uterus, Vagina, Fallopian Tube

Male reproductive system :

Urethra, Testicle, Penis, Prostate

Task 7.

a)

taste

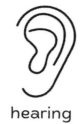
hearing

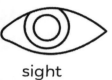
sight

touch

smell

b)
Touch – skin
Hearing – ear
Smell– nose
Sight – eye
Taste – tongue

Task 8.

a)

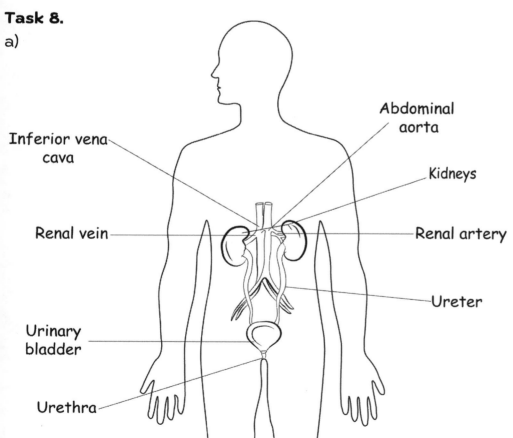

Inferior vena cava

Renal vein

Urinary bladder

Urethra

Abdominal aorta

Kidneys

Renal artery

Ureter

b)
Name of the system:
excretory system

Task 9.

a)

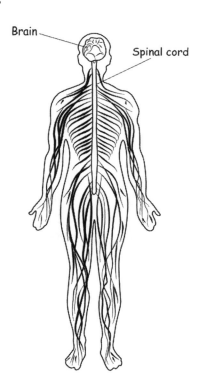

b)
Neurons

Task 10.

a)

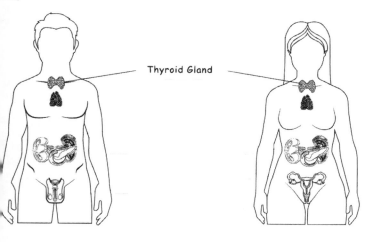

b)
The thyroid gland makes hormones and sends them out into the blood. These hormones affect how we digest and use food, how we feel, how much we weigh, and how our body temperature is controlled.

Task 11.

a)

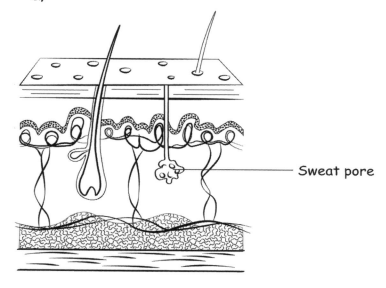

b)
- **Protection:** The skin protects the body from harmful things in the environment, like bacteria and UV radiation, by acting as a barrier.
- **Sensation:** The skin has nerve endings that help us feel heat, cold, pressure, and pain, among other things.

Thank You!

Want free goodies?!

E-MAIL US AT:

ana.roie.ruser@gmail.com

Made in the USA
Middletown, DE
27 November 2023

43718169R00077